The Holy Family in Egypt

The Holy Family in Egypt

Otto F. A. Meinardus

Illustrations by
George Onsy

THE AMERICAN UNIVERSITY IN CAIRO PRESS

First published as *In the Steps of the Holy Family from Bethlehem to Upper Egypt* by Dar al-Maaref, Cairo, 1963

This edition, with new illustrations, © 1986 by
The American University in Cairo Press
113 Sharia Kasr el Aini
Cairo, Egypt

Fifth printing 1997

Dar el Kutub No. 4604/85
ISBN 977 424 129 0

Printed in Egypt

Contents

Preface 7
1   Egypt at the time of the Visit of the Holy Family 9
       The Last Days of the Ptolemies 9
       Egypt as a Roman Province 11
2   The Flight of the Holy Family to Egypt 15
       The Birth of Christ 15
       From Bethlehem to the Nile Delta 20
       In the Nile Delta 26
       In the Nile Valley 35
3   The Return of the Holy Family to Palestine 61
    Bibliography and Acknowledgments 67

The Annunciation

Preface

The following history of the journey of the Holy Family to Egypt has been compiled from various Eastern and Western traditions. The material which I have used has been taken from the Apocryphal Gospels of Pseudo-Matthew and St. Thomas, as well as from several Infancy Gospels, especially the Arabic and Armenian ones. In addition to this apocryphal literature, I have made use of the *Vision of Theophilus* by the 23rd Patriarch of Alexandria (fourth century) and the Homily of Zachariah, Bishop of Sakha (seventh century). Furthermore, I have consulted the Coptic and Ethiopic Synaxaria, the writings of the thirteenth-century historians Abu 'l-Makarim and Solomon of Khirlat, several Muslim traditions, and finally the reports of the mediaeval pilgrims to the Holy Land who visited Egypt in the course of their pilgrimage. Wherever possible, I have given the local oral traditions and added them to the story.

The itinerary of the Holy Family, as set out in this small volume, is based chiefly on mediaeval traditions, which, however, are still considered part of the heritage of the Copts. Thus an attempted reconstruction of the itinerary of the Holy Family will, it is hoped, prove useful to the student of Christian Egypt.

I have tried to present the reader with a picture of first-century Egypt, though I am well aware that this is bound to have its shortcomings since the social and economic conditions in Egypt in the first century were inevitably other than those of the tenth to thirteenth centuries, to which most of the traditions relating to the Holy Family's visit to Egypt belong.

In order to make this study as complete as possible, I have visited those places in Egypt which, according to the various traditions, were hallowed by the presence of the Holy Family, and wherever possible I have given a brief description of these localities as they actually are. In this connection I wish to express my gratitude to Mr. Latif T. Ghobrial, M.A., who has been kind enough to accompany me on many field-trips through the Nile Delta and to Upper Egypt. With regard to the research work, Dr. O.H.E. Khs-Burmester has offered many helpful suggestions for which I am deeply grateful.

Portions of the second chapter have appeared in volume VII of the *Collectanea,* the annual publication of the Franciscan Centre of Oriental Christian Studies in Cairo.

Otto Meinardus

Feast of the Coming of our Lord into Egypt.
Bashons 24, 1678.
June 1, 1962

1
Egypt at the Time of the Visit of the Holy Family

The Last Days of the Ptolemies.

In the year 51 B.C., Cleopatra, the beautiful seventeen-year-old daughter of Ptolemy XI, ascended the ancient Pharaonic throne of Egypt. It was understood that after a few years, according to Ptolemaic custom, she was to marry her younger brother Ptolemy XIV. In 48 B.C. Ptolemy, wishing to be sole master of the state, banished his sister. Thus deprived of all royal authority, the charming Cleopatra withdrew to Syria, where she prepared to regain her rights by force of arms. The personal fascination for Cleopatra induced Julius Caesar to undertake a war on her behalf.

In the meantime however, Gnaeus Pompey, at one time triumvir and consul, and Rome-appointed guardian of the Egyptian rulers, saw his influence in Egypt endangered, and being jealous also of Julius Caesar's achievements in Gaul and elsewhere, he hurried to Egypt. Pompey's arrival in Egypt made it necessary for Ptolemy's council to decide whether to support Caesar or Pompey. Achillas and Lucius Septimus, the commanders of the Roman troops in Egypt, were sent to the city of Pelusium on the seacoast to welcome Pompey as a friend, and thus to murder him, which they effectively did.

Caesar attacked Egypt, and having secured Alexandria, reinstated Cleopatra as ruler of the land of the Pharaohs, and for a period of three years Cleopatra and her brother Ptolemy ruled as co-regents until the latter was poisoned at Cleopatra's orders. Returning with Julius Caesar to Rome, Cleopatra lived as his mistress until his assassination in 44 B.C., when she returned to Egypt. Subsequently she became the ally and mistress of Mark Antony. The *Caesar and Cleopatra* was followed by the *Antony and Cleopatra.*

Antony, infatuated with Cleopatra's charms, transferred several Roman territories to her dominion, for Cleopatra had always dreamed of restoring the ancient empire of her royal ancestors. Several times she travelled to Palestine where she attempted to captivate with her irresistible charm King Herod the Great. Herod, though much impressed with the queen's personal attractiveness, realized that any liaison with her would merely lead to enmity with Antony. Cleopatra, deeply distressed by Herod's aloofness, succeeded however in persuading Antony to order Herod to come to visit him in Alexandria. Herod, however, outwitted the Egyptian Queen. With gold and other gifts, the King of Judaea came to Alexandria to bribe and win over Antonius. In spite of this, Herod had to relinquish the coasts of Palestine to Cleopatra, and also the city of Jericho which was famous for its beautiful gardens and plantations. Here, according to Flavius Josephus, was the famous plantation of balsam trees which the Queen of Sheba had presented to King Solomon. Cleopatra transplanted some of these trees to Heliopolis, where they were cared for by Jewish gardeners from the Jordan valley. Some thirty years later, the Holy Family on their flight to Egypt sought refuge with these Jewish gardeners, who had been appointed by Cleopatra.

In 31 B.C., the Roman Senate dispatched a fleet under the command of Octavian. Antony's fleet supported by Egyptian ships under Cleopatra met that of Octavian off Actium on the coast of Greece. After the defeat of Antony's forces, Cleopatra escaped to Alexandria, where Antony joined her. Having no prospect of ultimate success, she accepted Octavian's proposal to assassinate Antony. She enticed her former lover to join her in a mausoleum which she had built in order that they might die together. Antony, in the mistaken belief that his mistress had already committed suicide, took his own life. Octavian refused, however, to yield to the beauty and attractions of Cleopatra. Rather than be led as captive in a Roman triumph, Cleopatra chose the alternative and applied an asp to her youthful bosom. Whatever her moral failings, Cleopatra was a woman of outstanding genius and a worthy opponent of Rome. As Idris Bell has well said, "Cleopatra's choice of the snake which was to give her release from captivity was significant. It was an asp, the Egyptian cobra, the sacred snake of Lower Egypt. As Pharaoh, Lord of the Two Lands, Cleopatra had worn the double crown, the vulture crown of Upper, the cobra crown of Lower Egypt. The cobra was the minister of the sun-god, whose bite conferred not only immortality but divinity. Cleopatra had taken the royal road to death and joined the company of the gods, and nothing remained for Octavian but to incorporate Egypt in the dominions of the Roman people."

Egypt as a Roman Province.
With the famous words "I added Egypt to the dominions of the Roman people", which Gaius Julius Caesar Octavianus Augustus records in the *Res Gestae,* an autobiography, Augustus, now sole ruler, sums up his expedition to Egypt. One of the first things which Augustus did was to order the destruction of all the statues of Antony, of which there were more than fifty. He entrusted the government of his new province, the greatest and richest of all the Roman provinces, to

a man of little note and talent, Cornelius Gallus, a friend of Virgil, and himself a poet; and this he did intentionally so as to avoid the possibility that a governor of this rich province might be tempted to aspire to the Roman Imperium.

Cornelius Tacitus mentions in his *Annals* that the Senate gave the command of the provinces to members of their own body only. This new province, the chief granary of the Empire, Augustus persuaded the Senate to confer on him. He appointed to it prefects of equestrian rank. These were answerable for their conduct to nobody but the emperor, who for the Egyptians was a new Pharaoh, "the Lord of the Two Lands", represented in the cartouches with the usual divine attributes. No Egyptian city was allowed to have a senate or municipal form of government; on the contrary, Augustus not only gave the command of Egypt to a man below the rank of senator, but also ordered that no senator should ever be allowed to set foot into Egypt.

At Alexandria, Augustus was visited by Herod, King of Judaea, who hastened to beg him to restore to him those portions of the kingdom which Antonius had bestowed upon Cleopatra. Augustus received him as a friend, and not only returned to him the territory which had been taken away from him, but also added the province of Samaria and the free cities on the coast.

The Greeks of Alexandria, jealous of the fact that the Jews had also the right of citizenship, urged the Emperor to retract this privilege. Augustus, however, who had no reason to agree to the petitions of the Greeks, granted the Jews the full privileges of the Hellenes. They were allowed their own magistrates and courts of justice with the free exercise of their own religion. The Hellenistic Jews in Egypt were indeed important, both on account of their numbers and their learning (*Acts* 9:6). It would have been among the Jewish colonists in Egypt that the Holy Family would have dwelt during their stay in this land.

The first step which Rome had to take with regard to her new province was to restore law and order in the country. Three legions and nine cohorts were stationed at Alexandria but there were detachments at various points up the Nile valley. Strabo states that one of the legions was stationed at Babylon, a fortress which about twenty years later was to offer shelter to the Holy Family. This military force was more than adequate, for when the people of Heroonpolis, a town of some military importance on the road to Palestine, revolted, and afterwards, when rebellion broke out in the Thebaid against the Roman taxcollectors, these risings were easily put down. As mentioned above, the supreme authority in the land was vested in the prefect, who at the same time was commander-in-chief of the troops, head of the civil, judicial and financial administration of Egypt. The old judicial system of itinerant courts was replaced by the *conventus* held periodically by the prefect at various places, for example at Pelusium for the nomes of the eastern Delta, at Alexandria for those of the western Delta, and at Memphis for the rest of Egypt. These periodical *conventus* were not merely confined to the trials and lawsuits, but also included the examination of the reports and accounts of the nome officials.

Following the governmental practice of the later Ptolemies, Augustus divided Egypt into three large districts, the Thebaid, Middle Egypt, and the Delta. These districts were governed by *epistrategoi,* who were purely administrative, and without any military power. Otherwise, the old division of Egypt into nomes was maintained, each administered by a *strategos.* The priests of the temples were required to submit to the *strategos* of the nome each year a return of personnel and property, as well as the annual temple-accounts. The sacred land still figured in the land registers, though a good deal of it was confiscated, and the temples were placed under stricter control than ever before. While curbing the material power of the priests, Augustus did not interfere with the observance of the local cults, and a considerable amount of building at several of the great temples in Upper Egypt is dated to his reign. We even know of sacred buildings which were dedicated in his name, such as the peribolos of a temple at Soknopaiou Nesos in the Fayyum.

The list of building activities under Augustus is a comparatively long one, especially if one considers the public works, such as the construction of the camp at Nikopolis, the repair of the cisterns on the road thence to the Red Sea, and the digging of a canal from Schedia to Alexandria. Strabo mentions that the clearing of the canals, which every year were more or less blocked up by the same mud which made the fields fruitful, was one of the greatest tasks of the Emperor in Egypt. The prefect Gaius Petronius employed the leisure of his soldiers on this wise and benevolent work. "Before the times of Petronius there was the greatest plenty, and the rise of the river was the greatest when it rose to the height of fourteen cubits, but when it rose to eight only, a famine ensued. During the government of Petronius (25-21 B.C.), however, when the Nile rose twelve cubits only, there was a most abundant crop, and once when it mounted to eight only, no famine followed."

This brief description shows that the Romans enforced a strong, centralized and well-supported administration. Yet in spite of their administrative ability and the numerous projects which they initiated and completed, Egypt under Roman Rule was a cow to be milked for the benefit of Rome. The land of the Pharaohs was ruined by shortsighted exploitation which eventually led to both economic and social decline. It was during this period that many towns and villages in Egypt were blessed by the visit of the Holy Family who, fleeing from the oppressive regime of King Herod of Judaea, sought refuge among the descendants of their Jewish ancestors in the Delta and the Nile Valley.

2
The Flight
of the Holy Family to Egypt

The Birth of Christ.

"And it came to pass in those days, that there went out a decree from Caesar Augustus, that all the world should be taxed" (*Luke* 2:1). This general census took place every fourteen years throughout the Roman empire, which included at that time also Egypt, Syria and Palestine. As regards the Roman province of Syria, "this taxing was first made when Cyrenius was governor of Syria" (*Luke* 2:2). Cyrenius, the governor, was the well-known Róman senator Publius Sulpicius Quirinius, who during the period between 10 B.C. and 7 B.C. commanded the legions in the war against the Homonadenses, a tribe of the Taurus Mountains in Asia Minor. During these three years Quirinius had his headquarters in Syria.

We have a record which indicates that a census was taken about the years 6 A.D. or 7 A.D. This census, however, cannot be that referred to by St. Luke, as the Evangelist clearly states that the first census took place at the time of the birth of Christ, while King Herod was still living, that is to say before 4 B.C.

In this connection it should be noted that in the change from the *Anno Urbis Conditae* (Roman Era) to *Anno Domini* (Christian Era) which was made by Dionysius Exiguus in 526 A.D., an error of four years occurred in his calculations. He placed the birth of Christ in the year 754 A.U.C. But Herod the Great, who slew the innocents of Bethlehem, died in April of the year 750 A.U.C.

Now, if we add the three and a half years residence of the Holy Family in Egypt (according to Coptic tradition) to the date of the death of King Herod (4 B.C.), we arrive at the date of 7 B.C. for the birth of Christ, which was the very period when Quirinius held office in Syria. Furthermore, if we count back fourteen years from the census made in 6 A.D. or 7 A.D., we discover the date of the first census in 7 B.C., the year of the birth of Christ.

"Now when Jesus was born in Bethlehem of Judaea in the days of Herod the King, behold, there came wise men from the east to Jerusalem, saying, Where is he that is born King of the Jews? For we have seen his star in the east, and are come to worship him" (*Matthew* 2:1-2).

With regard to this star, W. Keller writes in *The Bible as History*, that according to the calculations of Kepler and Schnabel, this particular phenomenon occurred in the year 7 B.C. In 1603, Johannes Kepler, the famous mathematician and astronomer, observed two planets, Saturn and Jupiter, which in the constellation of Pisces had moved so close to each other that they appeared almost like one single and unusually large star. Studying his notes, Kepler remembered having read in the writings of the Jewish philosopher Abravanel, that the Messiah would appear when there was a conjunction of Saturn and Jupiter in the constellation of Pisces. According to astronomical calculations, Kepler deduced that the same conjunction occurred in 7 B.C., the year in which Jesus Christ was born. In 1925, the German scholar P. Schnabel, while deciphering the Neo-Babylonian cuneiform inscriptions of the ancient School of Astrology at Sippar in Babylon, discovered a series of dates with regard to observations of planetary positions in the constellation of Pisces. Here, Jupiter and Saturn were carefully traced over a period of five months. The date, which Schnabel calculated, fell into the year 7 B.C. Furthermore, it was established that this conjunction was particularly clearly visible in the Mediterranean area. According to Chaldaean astrology, the constellation of Pisces was the sign of the 'West-country', the Mediterranean; and according to Jewish tradition, it was also the sign of Israel, the sign of the Messiah. Thus Keller writes: "This wonderful encounter of Jupiter and Saturn, guardian of Israel, in the constellation of the 'West-country', of the Messiah, must have deeply moved the Jewish astrologers of Babylon, for according to astrological ways of thinking, it pointed to the appearance of a mighty king in the west country, the land of their fathers. To experience that in person, to see it with their own eyes, that was the reason for the journey of the wise astronomers from the East."

Ⲣⲁϣⲓ ⲑⲉⲗⲏⲗ ⲱ ⲭⲏⲙⲓ ⲛⲉⲙⲛⲉⲥϣⲏⲣⲓ
ⲛⲉⲙⲛⲉⲥⲑⲱϣ ⲧⲏⲣⲟⲩ ⲝⲉⲁϥⲓ ϣⲁⲣⲟ ⲛϫⲉ -
ⲡⲓⲙⲁⲓⲣⲱⲙⲓ ⲫⲏ ⲉⲧϣⲟⲡ ϧⲁϫⲱⲟⲩ ⲛⲛⲓⲉⲱⲛ
ⲧⲏⲣⲟⲩ ·

Be glad and rejoice, O Egypt; and her sons and all her borders, for there hath come to Thee the Lover of man, He Who is before all the ages.
Doxology for the Feast of the Entry of Our Lord into the Land of Egypt.
Bashons 24.

Places referred to on the map
and their corresponding ancient names

Ahnassiah	*Herakleopolis*
Ashmunain	*Hermopolis Magna*
Bahnasa	*Oxyrhynchus*
Beni Hassan	*Speos Artemidos*
Bikha Iysous	*(?) Sakha*
Bilbais	*Phelbes*
Farama	*Pelusium*
Gebel 't-Tair	*Akhoris*
Matariyah	*Heliopolis*
Mit Sammanud	*Sebennytos*
Musturud	*al-Mahammah*
Old Cairo	*Babylon*
Qusia	*Cusae*
Samalut	*Cynopolis*
Sanabu	*Pepleu*
Suez	*Clysma*
Tell al-Bastah	*Bubastis*
Terranah	*Terenuthis*
Wadi 'n-Natrun	*Scetis*

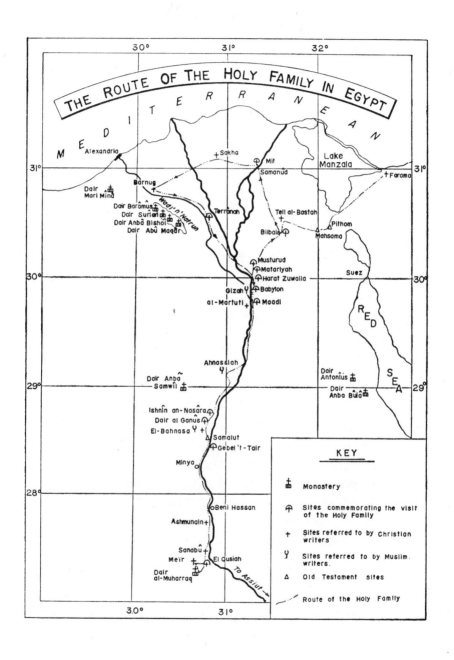

THE ROUTE OF THE HOLY FAMILY IN EGYPT

MEDITERRANEAN

30°   31°   32°

Alexandria

31°   Sakha   Mit   Lake   31°
                                    Samanud   Manzala   Farama

Dair   Barnug
Mari Mina

Dair Barâmus   Terrânah   Tell al-Bastah
Dair Suriân   Pithom
Dair Anbâ Bishoi   Bilbais   Mahsama
Dair Abû Maqâr

                                    Musturud
                                    Matariyah
30°   Harat Zuwaila   Suez   30°
                    Gizah   Babylon
                    al-Martuti   Maadi

                                                RED

                    Ahnassiah

                                                Dair
Dair Anba   Antonius   SEA
Samwil   29°
29°   Dair
                                                Anba Bûla

Ishnin an-Nasâra
Dair al-Ganûs
El-Bahnasa
                    Samalut
                    Gebel 't-Tair

            Minya

28°
                    Beni Hassan

Ashmunain

        Sanabû
    Meïr   El Qusiah
Dair   To Assiut
al-Muharraq

        3.0°   31°

KEY

♁   Monastery

♁   Sites commemorating the visit
     of the Holy Family

✝   Sites referred to by Christian
     writers

Ψ   Sites referred to by Muslim
     writers.

Δ   Old Testament sites

     Route of the Holy Family

From Bethlehem to the Nile Delta

"And when they [the wise men from the east] were departed, behold, the angel of the Lord appeareth to Joseph in a dream, saying, Arise, and take the young child and his mother, and flee into Egypt, and be thou there until I bring thee word: for Herod will seek the young child to destroy him. When he arose, he took the young child and his mother by night, and departed into Egypt: And was there until the death of Herod: that it might be fulfilled which was spoken of the Lord by the Prophet, saying, Out of Egypt have I called my son" (*Matt.* 2:13-15).

Before the Holy Family together with Salome, the midwife, departed from Bethlehem, they remained for a while in a grotto, which is situated south-east of the Basilica of the Nativity. This grotto, known to the Arabs as *Magharat as-Saiyidah,* the Grotto of the Lady, is an ancient sanctuary which is venerated by Christians and Muslims alike. An Armenian tradition relates that the Blessed Virgin Mary on her flight to Egypt stopped here and suckled her Child. Some drops of her milk fell on the rock, and it immediately turned white. There is good reason to believe that a church was built on this site by St. Paula, who lived in Bethlehem and died there in 404 A.D. Though at first dedicated to the Virgin Mother, the church was later known as that of St. Paula. In the fourteenth century it belonged to the Greeks and was dedicated to St. Nicholas, and eventually it passed into Latin hands. This grotto has supplied those soft white stones, known as *Virgin's Milk,* which can be found in many Latin churches throughout Europe. The present church built over the Grotto was dedicated in 1872. The Grotto is a favourite place of pilgrimage for women on account of the milk-white rock, which is prized for its healing power and as an aid to lactation. Women pilgrims take away with them pieces of this soft rock, which having ground into powder, they mix with water and drink.

In connection with the Flight into Egypt, it would not be out of place to mention the most likely means of transport

The angel's warning to Joseph

which the Holy Family used. Both the Eastern and Western traditions are unanimous that the journey of the Holy Family in Egypt was accomplished by ass. In this case, the Blessed Virgin would have been seated on the ass, holding the Divine Child in her arms, and Joseph would have walked at their side leading the ass. Such for example was the means of transport used by Moses, when he took his wife and his sons, and set them upon an ass and returned to Egypt (*Exodus* 4:20). Furthermore, the prophecy of Zechariah stated explicitly that the Messiah would come riding upon an ass (*Zech.* 9:9). Apart, however, from Biblical analogy and prophecy, the ass was the animal most frequently used in the East for travel. Indeed, the ass was one of the most valuable possessions of a family. In comparison to a horse, an ass is much more economical, for it can be given almost anything to eat. As a skilled worker, Joseph the Carpenter could certainly have afforded to purchase an ass. This, according to Jewish custom would probably have been adorned with an amulet consisting of a fox's tail or a crimson plume to protect it from the evil eye.

To depict the Holy Family as clad in the Arab dress of recent times, namely, the *qamis* (a sort of long shirt), the *'abayah* (a top-robe), the *kuffiyah* (a scarf) and the *'uqal* (a head-dress), is just as incorrect as to clothe them in the garments of the mediaeval painters. The clothes which the Holy Family would have worn would have been those in fashion at the time in the whole Graeco-Roman world. These, which were the same for men as for women, consisted of the *linea* (a long robe reaching from the neck to the feet) with close-fitting sleeves, the *tunica* (a sort of tunic reaching to the knees) with short sleeves, the *planeta* or *casula* (a large round piece of stuff with a hole in the centre for the head to pass through) which fell in folds over the shoulders and arms and enveloped the whole body down to the knees. It was an out-door garment and afforded warmth and protection against the wind and rain. For travel and work a girdle was added, and for travel shoes or sandals were worn. Incidentally, these three garments, the *linea,* the *tunica* and the *planeta* or *casula* became ultimately the ecclesiastical vestments known as the alb, the tunicle and the chasuble. With regard to the food eaten by the Holy Family on their travels, this would have consisted (in addition to meat, fish and bread) of coarse horse-beans, lentils, chickpeas, cucumbers, onions, garlic and leeks. The fruits available at this period and in the Near East would have been grapes, dates and figs, and honey would have replaced the modern sugar. Wine "that maketh glad the heart of man" (*Ps.* 104:15) was a common beverage.

According to the *Armenian Infancy Gospel,* the Holy Family first went to the ancient Philistine city and seaport of Ashkelon, where Samson went to kill thirty Philistines (*Judges* 14:19). At the time of the visit of the Holy Family, Ashkelon was a strong and beautiful centre of Hellenistic culture with a special cult to Dercetus or Atargates, a goddess with the body of a fish and the face of a woman. Herod the Great had embellished the city with fountains and sumptuous buildings, of which some beautiful Corinthian columns can be seen to this day.

From Ashkelon the Holy Family proceeded in an almost easterly direction to Hebron, one of the oldest towns in the world. According to the Bible, the city was founded seven years before Zoan (*Num.* 13:22), the present village of San al-Hagar in Lower Egypt. Hebron's chief interest is now its Haram, an enclosure built over the traditional site of the cave of Machpelah (*Gen.* 23). Within the enclosure is a mosque and a synagogue, formerly a twelfth-century Crusaders' church, which in its turn was built on the site of a basilica of Justinian's time. Within the building are the cenotaphs of Abraham, Isaac, Jacob, Sarah, Rebecca and Leah. The *Armenian Infancy Gospel* informs us that the Holy Family remained here in hiding for a period of six months.

About forty kilometres further on, in a westerly direction,

there is the site of the ancient Canaanite stronghold of Gaza (*Gen.* 10:19). If the Holy Family had followed the caravan-route from Judaea to Egypt, they would have passed this city, into which Samson was enticed and finally overcome by the beautiful Delilah (*Judges* 16:21-31). At the time of Christ, this city had acquired a certain amount of splendour and magnificence, as it had become a centre of Hellenistic culture, for after its destruction by Alexander Jannaeus, brother of Aristobulus I, in 94 B.C., the Roman Consul Aulus Gabinus had rebuilt it in 57 B.C.

By taking the route which runs parallel to the shore of the Mediterranean Sea, the Holy Family would have crossed, after another two hours, the Wadi Gaza. It was here that Sir Flinders Petrie carried out his excavations on the presumed site of Gerar. Here also, Abimelech, King of Gerar, took Sarah the wife of Abraham under the impression that she was his sister, as he himself said, but later he restored her to her husband (*Gen.* 15:1-16). When Isaac sojourned in Gerar, the people of the land desired Rebecca, his wife, but Abimelech protected both Isaac and Rebecca (*Gen.* 26:1-25).

A day's journey from Gaza brought the Holy Family to the ancient township of Jenysos, which is mentioned by Herodotus, the Greek historian. To-day, this village, which is part of the Gaza-strip, is known as Khan Yunis.

The next town on the Holy Family's route would have been Raphia (Rafah), the frontier-town between the Gaza-strip and the province of Egypt. Raphia, which had been the battleground of the contending forces of Ptolemy IV and Antiochus the Great in 217 B.C., was conquered by Alexander Jannaeus, the Maccabee and annexed to Judaea. It was restored again, however, to Egypt by Gabinus. During the Byzantine period, Raphia, like Gaza, was the seat of a bishop.

Continuing the caravan-route for another 44 km., about two days of travelling, the Holy Family crossed the River of Egypt, the Wadi al-'Arish, which at all times formed the natural

24

boundary between Egypt and Palestine. Strangely enough, what the ancients called the 'River of Egypt' was not the mighty Nile, but a small stream. By crossing this inconspicuous trickle, the Holy Family must have thought of the many occasions in the history of their people, when this 'brook of Egypt', with its "goings out" at the sea, served as boundary, from the days of the conquest of Canaan (*Num.* 34:5), to the calling of Solomon's assembly (*I Kings* 8:65). A little further on, the Holy Family would have arrived at the city of Rhinocolura, the present al-'Arish. Criminals and those accused of high treason were sent to this city to receive their punishment, which consisted in cutting off their noses.

Since we possess no evidence either written or oral as to the exact route followed by the Holy Family in their flight from Bethlehem to Egypt, the particulars given above are purely conjectural, but we may reasonably suppose that once the Holy Family were out of danger of pursuit, they would have travelled along the usual caravan route between Judaea and Egypt, which passed through towns and villages where they could have obtained food and shelter.

The first town which would be reached after Rhinocolura, was Ostrakini. Of this place we know very little beyond the fact that Abraham, Bishop of Ostrakini, attended the Oecumenical Council of Ephesus in 431 A.D. As a town, Ostrakini has disappeared, though there is a village called Straki, which is situated in the vicinity of al-'Arish.

Almost at the south-western end of the caravan-route from Judaea to Egypt there is the celebrated city of Pelusium (Farama), metropolis of the province of Augustamnica, sea-port and key to Egypt. To this city, which is identified with the Biblical Tahpanihes, Johanan, the son of Kareah (588 B.C.), "took the remnant of Judah... men and women, and children, and the king's daughters, and every person that Nebuzaradan the captain of the guard, had left with Gedaliah, and Jeremiah the prophet" (*Jer.* 43:5-8). Sixty-three years later, in 525 B.C.,

Psammetichos III was defeated at Pelusium by Cambyses the King of Persia, and Egypt became a Persian province. At the time of the Holy Family's visit, Pelusium was still an important city and seaport, and it is quite likely that they stopped here to rest for several days before entering the Nile Delta. Pelusium had many marshes lying around it, which, at the time of the Holy Family's visit, were called Barathra or water holes and swamps. For that matter, Pelusium may have received its name from the mud (*pelou*) of the swamps. The Greek monk Epiphanius (ninth century), as well as Bernard the Wise (870 A.D.), mentions the tradition according to which the Holy Family visited this historical city, which Maqrizi reckoned among the wonders of Egypt. In the *Itinerarium Bernardi Monachi* we read: "From Tamnis we came to the city of Faramea, where is a church of St. Mary, on the spot to which by the admonition of the angel, Joseph fled with the child and its mother. In this city, there is a multitude of camels, which are hired from the natives by the travellers to carry their baggage across the desert (to Jerusalem) which is a journey of six days." That many of the pilgrims passed through Farama is attested by the itineraries of men like Jacques de Vitry (1180 A.D.) and Marino Sanuto (1321 A.D.). Abu 'l-Makarim considered that "Farama was exceedingly wonderful, and one of the most ancient foundations of which there is a record. There were at Farama many churches and monasteries which were wrecked by the Persians and the Arabs." This city, indeed, was occupied by 'Amr ibn al-'As on his way to conquer Egypt. Subsequently, it was fortified again by al-Mutawakkil about 853 A.D. In 1117 A.D. Baldwin, King of Jerusalem, occupied the city, but unable to hold it, he laid it in ruins. Baedeker speaks of the ruined Tell Farama, which now contains no objects of interest.

In the Nile Delta.
It was at the time when Gaius Turranius (7 B.C.-4 B.C.) was Roman Prefect of Egypt, that the Holy Family crossed the narrow isthmus at al-Qantara (the bridge), which separates the

26

Lake Menzaleh from the Lake Balah. It was over this isthmus that the ancient caravan-route from Judaea to Egypt passed, a route which centuries before had been used by Abraham (*Gen.* 12:10) and Jacob and his sons (*Gen.* 16). In the steps of the patriarchs, the Holy Family entered the Province of Goshen.

By the land of Goshen (*Gen.* 45:10) we are to understand approximately the triangle of land which has as its apex the modern town of Zagazig, and as its base Bilbais and Tell al-Kebir. However, as the City of Pithom, the site of which is marked by the mounds near al-Mahsama, was also in the land of Goshen, the Wadi Tumilat must likewise have formed part of Goshen. Moreover, both the Septuagint Version of the Old Testament and Flavius Josephus add On, that is to say Heliopolis, to Pithom and Raamses, the fortified cities built by the Hebrews for Pharaoh (*Ex.* 1:11). If On really lay in Goshen, this would extend the district in which the Hebrews lived almost to the outskirts of the present City of Cairo. It should be remembered that it was Asenath, a daughter of a priest of On, whom Joseph married (*Gen.* 41:45).

The *Armenian Infancy Gospel* mentions that the Holy Family made their way into the Province of Goshen by passing through the Plain of Tanis, and that they settled in Bilbais, where they remained for a while. This tradition would suggest an alternative route, following the ancient Roman military road from al-Qantara via Faqus to Bilbais. At the same time, it would be most unlikely that the Holy Family passed as far north as Tanis, the Biblical Zoan (*Ps.* 87:12,43) and the present fishing village of San al-Hagar.

There is good reason to assume that the Holy Family entered the Nile Delta through the Wadi Tumilat, and if this were the case, one of the first towns which they would have reached on their way would have been Pithom or Pi-tum, the abode of Tum, the Setting Sun. We read in *Exodus* 1:11, that the Children of Israel in the land of Goshen built for Pharaoh the treasure cities Pithom and Raamses. (The LXX has "fortified, strong cities"). These military store-houses were evidently built by Ramses II, the Pharaoh of the Oppression, using for their construction Nile mud mixed with chopped straw. The ruins of Tell al-Maskuta, near al-Mahsama, mark the site of the Biblical Pithom. This site was excavated for the Egypt Exploration Fund by Professor Naville in 1883, who discovered among the temple-buildings several grain-stores.

The assumption that the Holy Family went through the Wadi Tumilat is supported by a Spanish tradition, supposedly told by King Sancho IV, el Bravo (1257-1295), at the time of the conquest of Tarifa. This story affirms the route which the Holy Family took along the coast of the Mediterranean. According to this Spanish tradition, the Holy Family was accompanied by a virgin (presumably Salome) and three young men. (One is tempted to see in these three young men a reference to the Three Holy Children in the Furnace or the Three Celestial Visitors to Abraham).

Because of the heat, however, the Holy Family decided to look for shelter in a cave. But as they approached a cave, a dragon came out of it and began to scream when it saw the Christ child. Thereupon, the dragon fell down and worshipped the Child. At the same time many lions and other wild animals joined the Holy Family. At first, the Holy Virgin was much frightened, but Jesus pacified his Mother and all the wild animals dwelt together and the prophecy of Isaiah was fulfilled which said: "The wolf also shall dwell with the lamb, and the leopard shall lie down with the kid; and the calf and the young lion and the fatling together; and a little child shall lead them" (*Isaiah* 11:6). Then the Holy Family proceeded further and Joseph saw a palm tree which provided shade for the weary travellers, and the palm tree bent down and offered its fruits to the Holy Virgin. When the Holy Family entered the province of Hieropolis, they came to a town called Sieno.

If we accept Hieropolis to be the ancient Heroopolis, the Holy Family would have passed through the Wadi Tumilat.

Christ pacifying the wild animals at the cave

Heroopolis or Abu Keyshed is the site of the ruins of Tell al-Maskuta. As to Sieno, this word has such a Spanish form that it will be difficult to discover beneath its dress the Egyptian name of the city.

On their way through the Wadi Tumilat, the Holy Family must have seen the byblus (papyrus) and the Egyptian bean which at that time grew in the marshes and lakes. The byblus, though not cultivated, could be seen especially in the lower parts of the Nile Delta. From the Egyptian bean, the ciborium, a kind of drinking cup was made, which could be found in great abundance in the shops in Alexandria and elsewhere, where they were sold as drinking vessels.

About fifteen kilometres westward of the ancient Pithom, there was situated the township of Succoth, the first halt of the Israelites on their exodus from Egypt (*Ex.* 12:37, 13:20). This site is generally identified with the village of al-Qassasin. A day's journey from Succoth would have brought the Holy Family to the other treasure city built by the Children of Israel, Raamses, the present village of Tell al-Kebir.

At Raamses, the Holy Family entered the fertile Nile Delta. Travelling further on in a westerly direction, they passed the ancient city of Pi-Sopt, the present village of Saft al-Hinna, and from thence they went to Bubastis, the Pi-Beseth of the Bible (*Ezekiel* 30:17,18). Most probably, the court where Joseph had his headquarters was at Bubastis. This city, of which only the ruins remain at the present day, must have been very important in the past. The deity of Bubastis was the great goddess Bast, who is represented with a disk encircled by a uraeus on her head and holding a lotus-sceptre in one hand. The festivals of Bast were celebrated with great rejoicings. Herodotus provides us with some very intimate knowledge regarding these festivities. "Now, when they are being conveyed to the city of Bubastis, they act as follows: for men and women embark together, and a great number of sexes in every barge, some of the women have castanets on which they play, and the men

30

play on the flute during the whole voyage, the rest of the women and men sing and clap their hands together at the same time... some dance, others stand up and behave in an unseemly manner... When they arrive at Bubastis, they celebrate the feast, offering up great sacrifices, and more wine is consumed at this festival than in all the rest of the year. What with men and women, besides children, they congregate, as the inhabitants say, to the number of seven hundred thousand" (*Herodotus, Bk. II,* 60).

According to the *Coptic Synaxarium,* Basatah (Bubastis, Pi-Beseth, Bastah or Tell al-Bastah), which is two kilometres south-west of Zagazig, was the first town in the Delta which the Holy Family and Salome visited. They were not, however, well received here in spite of the fact that they revealed a spring of water, which became a source of healing for all, except for the inhabitants of Basatah. Details of this story are given in the *Vision of Theophilus,* where we read that in Basatah, the Holy Family met two brigands, Titus, who was an Egyptian, and Dumachus, a Syrian. And the Syrian brigand said to the Egyptian: "I should have liked to plunder the garments that are on this woman and her Son, because they resemble the garments of kings, and if I had encountered them in a place other than this, I would have taken those garments from them." But the Egyptian brigand said to him: "Let us proceed on our way. I never saw a Child like this since I was born." Then Jesus asked for water and the Blessed Virgin looked around and did not find the water which her Son was asking for. Then the Blessed Virgin arose, and took her Son and brought Him to the town and asked the women for water to give to Him, but none of them wished to give them anything, as the inhabitants of that town had little compassion. When the brigands saw the Blessed Virgin and her Son entering Basatah, they came back and went to Joseph, and while he was asleep, they abducted the golden and silver sandals of Jesus and fled. When the Blessed Virgin realized this, she was much distressed and wept.

31

When Jesus however saw His Mother weeping, He wiped off her tears, and stretched His small finger and made the sign of the cross on the earth, and instantly a spring of water jetted forth and flowed on the ground. And they drank this water which was as sweet as honey and as white as snow. Then Jesus blessed this water and said: "Let this water help make whole and heal the souls and bodies of all those who shall drink of it, with the exception of the inhabitants of this town, of whom none shall be healed by it."

The Copts remember the town of Basatah also because of St. Apoli, the son of Justus Stratelates, who was beaten and flogged at Basatah during the persecution of the Emperor Diocletian (284-305 A.D.). Finally, St. Apoli was cast into prison, where Jesus appeared to him by night and consoled him.

Today, the ruins of the ancient Bubastis with their brick walls are the only remains of this once famous city. The temple of the goddess Bast at the south-west foot of the hill was excavated in 1887-89 by Professor Naville.

Disappointed at their reception in Basatah, the Holy Family went on a day's journey further southward, and reached the town of Bilbais, by which passes the modern Ismailiya Canal. As the Holy Family entered the town, a funeral procession came out, and Jesus, who had compassion on the mourners, raised the dead man to life. Then He learned that it was the son of a widow, who having been brought back to life, declared: "This is the True God, the Saviour of the world, Who is born of the Blessed Virgin, Who accomplished a mystery which the human intellect cannot comprehend." And all the inhabitants of Bilbais believed in Jesus.

During the Middle Ages, the pilgrims to the Holy Places, who passed through Egypt, stopped at Bilbais to kneel at the foot of the great tree, which according to both Christians and Muslims, commemorates the stay of the Holy Family at Bilbais. The Muslims called it the Tree of the Virgin, and they had such respect for it that they reserved the space around the tree as a necropolis for their venerated saints. They relate with sorrow that the soldiers of Napoleon who passed by this tree wanted to cut it down, but at the first blow of the axe, it began to bleed, and they departed in fear. The tree was eventually cut down about 1850 by some workers who used the wood to make a fire.

Today, there is only one Coptic church in Bilbais, the Church of St. George (*Mari Girgis*) which is situated in the north eastern part of the town, about one kilometre from the main road. The site which commemorates the visit of the Holy Family to Bilbais is the 'Uthman ibn al-Haris al-Ansari Mosque, in the centre of the town, at the corner of Sharia al-Ansari and Sharia al-Baghdadi.

According to the *Ethiopic and Coptic Synaxaria,* the Holy Family left the Sharqiah Province and pursued their way in a northerly direction till they reached the town of Samannud (Gamnudi), the ancient Sebennytos or Zeb-nuter, which is situated on the Damietta branch of the Nile, where they crossed the river towards the west. A local tradition in Samannud relates that the present Church of Apa Nub was built on the ruins of an ancient church dedicated to the Blessed Virgin, which in its turn was built on the site where the Holy Family stayed. The Christians of Samannud point to a place in the nave of the church where at one time there was a well, the water of which had been blessed by Jesus. The relics of the martyr are preserved in this church, whither every year about a thousand pilgrims flock on July 31st, the feast of the saint. Apa Nub, who was a native of Nahisah, went to Lysias, the Governor of Samannud, and professed that he was a Christian. He was then taken away on board a ship and crucified to the mast, but was afterwards miraculously released. At length Armenius, the Governor of Alexandria, had him put to death.

In his *Homily,* Zachariah, the seventh-century Coptic Bishop of Sakha, states that the Holy Family proceeded from Samannud to Burullus, near the Mediterranean coast. Here, at the Shrine of St. Dimianah, the Antonian monks relate an oral tradition of the visit of the Holy Family to the area, which three centuries later was blessed by the blood of the martyrdom of the virgin saint Dimianah and her forty virgins. The large crowds of pilgrims, who, every year from the 5th to the 22nd of May, come from all over Egypt and assemble at the Shrine of St. Dimianah, know little or nothing of the tradition of the visit of the Holy Family. They come because of the intercessions of Sitt Dimianah, the daughter of the governor, who supposedly appears annually in some form or another to the multitude of the faithful.

Having crossed the Damietta branch of the Nile, the Holy Family travelled westwards to al-Gharbiyah, the province which is situated between the Rosetta and Damietta branches of the Nile. On the way, Jesus put His foot upon a stone, and the mark of the sole of His foot remained upon the stone, and the place became known as Bikha Isous, that is to say, the footprint of Jesus. I have been unable to locate this place, which is mentioned by the *Ethiopic and Coptic Synaxaria.* It has been suggested that Basus may be a contraction of the name Bikha Isous, but it is most unlikely that Bikha Isous should be identified with the village of Basus which lies between Cairo and Qalyub, as stated by Amelineau. Dr. Murad Kamil suggests that Bikha Isous might be the town of Sakha, famous for its pillar on which St. Agathon the Stylite (seventh century) stood for fifty years. Sakha is situated in the province of Gharbiyah, about two kilometres south of Kafr ash-Shaikh. This suggestion might be supported by pointing to a confusion of the Arabic orthography of the two names. Indeed, if the diacritical points were omitted, the Arabic word ligatures of Sakha and Bikha show distinct similarities.

After Bikha Isous, the Holy Family travelled westwards and crossed the river, probably the Rosetta branch of the Nile. Continuing their journey, they saw from afar the Desert of Scetis, the Wadi 'n-Natrun, and Jesus blessed it and said to His

Mother: "Know, O my Mother, that in this desert there shall live many monks, ascetes and spiritual fighters, and they shall serve God like angels." Though there is no tradition to support it, the Holy Family would most probably have seen the Desert of Scetis from the town of Terranah, the ancient bishopric of Terenouti, fifteen kilometres north of al-Khatatba. Terranah, which is situated on the Rosetta branch of the Nile, is the town which is nearest to the Desert of Scetis, actually about forty kilometres from the Monastery of St. Macarius (Dair Abu Maqar). Today there are only four monasteries left in the Wadi 'n-Natrun, namely the Monastery of the Romans (Dair al-Baramus), the Monastery of the Syrians (Dair as-Surian), the Monastery of St. Bishoi (Dair Anba Bishoi) and the Monastery of St. Macarius, which is dedicated to the famous St. Macarius who is honoured among the founders of monasticism in both the East and the West. In 1986 there were about 320 monks occupying the four Wadi 'n-Natrun monasteries.

In the Nile Valley.
Continuing their journey southward, the Holy Family eventually reached the city of On or the Biblical Bethshemesh (*Jer.* 43:13). At the time of Strabo, about sixteen years before the visit of the Holy Family to On or Heliopolis, the city was entirely deserted, not having recovered from the destruction which it incurred at the time of the Persian invasion (525 B.C.). However, various temples and buildings of historical interest were still standing and were pointed out to Strabo by the dragoman of that time. The Holy Family would have naturally avoided lodging in this deserted pagan city, and in consequence they sought some dwelling place nearby in which there would most likely have been Jewish families living on account of its proximity to the Jewish centre at Leontopolis. Thus they halted at the site of the present village of Matariyah, now a suburb of Cairo. The visit to Matariyah is not only well attested by the *Apocryphal Gospel of Pseudo-Matthew* and the *Coptic and Ethiopic Synaxaria,* but also it is mentioned by the

mediaeval pilgrims to the Holy Land. According to the *Ethiopic Synaxarium,* when the Holy Family approached Matariyah, there was a staff in the hand of Joseph wherewith he used to smite Jesus, but Joseph gave Him the staff. Then said Jesus unto his mother: 'We will tarry here', and that place and its desert and the well became known as Matariyah. And Jesus took Joseph's staff, and broke it into little pieces, and planted these pieces in that place, and He dug with His own Divine hands a well, and there flowed from it sweet water, which had an exceeding sweet odour. And Jesus took some of the water in His hands, and watered therewith the pieces of wood which He had planted, and straightway they took root, and put forth leaves, and an exceedingly sweet perfume was emitted by them, which was sweeter than any other perfume. And these pieces of wood grew and increased and they called them 'balsam'. And Jesus said unto His Mother, 'O My Mother, these Balsam, which I have planted, shall abide here for ever, and from them shall be taken the oil for Christian baptism when they baptize in the name of the Father, and the Son and the Holy Ghost.'

The *Apocryphal Gospel of Pseudo-Matthew* replaces the balsam with a palm tree, a tradition which is also preserved in the Quran. According to the Quranic version, the Blessed Virgin saw a palm tree and wished to rest under it. When she was seated there, she saw fruit on it, and she said to Joseph that she would like to have some. Then Jesus, sitting in His Mother's lap, with a joyful countenance, bade the palm tree to give to His Mother of its fruit. The tree bent as low as her feet, and she gathered as much as she wanted. He bade it to rise again and give to them of the water concealed below its roots. A spring came forth, and all rejoiced and drank thereof. The *I Infancy Gospel* adds that when the Blessed Virgin had washed the swaddling clothes of Jesus and had hung them out to dry upon a post, a boy possessed with the devil took one of them down and put it upon his head. And presently the devil began

The Holy Tree at Matariyah

to come out of his mouth and fly away in the shape of crows and serpents. From that time, the boy was healed by the power of Jesus, and he began to sing praises and give thanks to the Lord who had healed him.

The village of Matariyah enjoyed great popularity among the pilgrims to the Holy Land. This blessed site must have appeared like a paradise to these pilgrims who had crossed the desert from Mount Sinai, for the well with its beautiful surroundings was a resort for such wealthy Mamelukes as the Emir Yashbak, who built a domed house here in which, from time to time, he entertained his master and friend Qait Bey (1467-1496). Entrance to the garden cost the pilgrims six ducats for which sum they could enjoy relaxation and bathing in the pool, the waters of which both Christians and Muslims believed to be holy and medicinal. The Dominican Friar Felix Fabri (1480) noticed close to the gate an immense fig tree. In its hollow trunk, as in a small chapel, two lamps hung, for the tree had once opened to provide refuge for the Blessed Virgin. There was a tradition that the Holy Family was pursued by two brigands, and that the tree miraculously opened to conceal them. According to Pero Tafur (1435-1439) only five pilgrims at a time were permitted to enter the Garden of Balm, and none was allowed to pinch or nip off leaves or twigs to take away with them. The reason for this protective policy may be explained by the fact that the earlier pilgrims were in the habit of depleting the balm-trees. Indeed, Burchard of Mount Sion (1285-1295) records that he went to Matariyah and carried off much balsam wood and bathed in the well which waters the garden, wherein the Blessed Virgin had dipped her Son. All the pilgrims are unanimous in their observation that the Garden of Balsam was tilled by Christians only. Ludoph von Suchem (1336) saw among the Christian guardians four Germans, one from Schwartzenburg, who had been a renegade, and another, a one-eyed man named Nicholas, who was a very good man, as the Christian captives bore witness. The balm was either obtained from the fruit of the bush or by boiling the branches. It was used medicinally and also in the concoction of the Chrism which is used at Baptism. The Muslims recommended its use for nasal trouble, lumbago or pain in the knee, while the Christians prescribed it for snake-bites, toothache and poisonings.

As a recognition of their share, the Sultan was accustomed to give to the two Christian patriarchs a portion of balm. Thus when De Lannoy (1421) was in Egypt, the Patriarch of the Copts was able to present to him, as Ambassador of France, a phial of pure balm.

Felix Fabri explained the presence of the bushes of balm at Matariyah by quoting Flavius Josephus, according to whom the Queen of Sheba had presented them to King Solomon, and that they had blossomed in the Holy Land until they were transplanted by Augustus Caesar to Matariyah. But Fabri was confident of one thing, namely that the plants never flourished until the visit of the Holy Family. There was a general belief that the balsam trees could not produce the balsam without the water of the spring. It is said that the Sultan al-Malik al-Kamil (1218-1238) once asked his father, al-'Adil, to plant some of the trees in a neighbouring plot of land, but there they did not blossom. Thereupon he received the permission to irrigate the trees with the water of the well of the Blessed Virgin, and consequently the trees revived and brought forth an abundant crop. Marino Sanuto (1321) and John Poloner (1421) believed that they had seen the actual palm tree which had bowed itself to the Blessed Virgin, that she might gather dates from it, and had then raised itself up again. When the heathens saw this, so Sanuto remarks, they cut down the palm tree, but it joined itself together again the following night. The marks of the cutting were still seen at the time of his pilgrimage.

The balsam shrubs have long since disappeared. The sycamore tree which now stands at Matariyah was planted in 1672. The fall of this venerable tree, due to old age, took place on June 14, 1906, but fortunately a living shoot from it remains to this day.

From Matariyah the Holy Family went to a locality where now stands the Church of the Blessed Virgin in the Harat Zuwaila of Cairo. It is situated in the north east district of Cairo, at the end of a lane leading off the Sharia Bain as-Surain, and was probably first erected in the tenth century. From the fourteenth century to the year 1660 it served as the patriarchal church in Cairo. The lower church is dedicated to the Blessed Virgin, and the upper church to St. George. In the north west corner of the lower church a doorway gives access to another church, which is dedicated to St. Mercurius. Annexed to the Church of the Blessed Virgin of the Harat Zuwaila there is a convent of nuns. The nuns of this convent relate the tradition that when the Holy Family rested at this locality, Jesus blessed the water of the well, and the Blessed Virgin drank from it. This well is situated in the floor before the southern sanctuary of the lower church, and the water is still used for healing the sick. Every year on the day of the feast of the consecration of the first Church of the Blessed Virgin at Philippi (June 20th), Ethiopian priests come to take some water of this well. According to the nuns, they drink it and wash themselves with it, a common practice among Eastern Christians as regards holy water.

Continuing their way southwards, the Holy Family passed the Fortress of Babylon (Old Cairo) which commanded the route to Upper Egypt and where they halted on their return to Palestine. They would have certainly seen the triangular pyramids of Gizah which may have seemed to them, as to the pilgrims several centuries later, to be Joseph's granaries. At the time of their visit, two of these pyramids, the Cheops and the Chefren pyramid, were reckoned among the seven wonders of the world. According to al-Hafiz Abu Bakr ben Thabet al-Khatib who had received the tradition from Nabit ben Sharit, there used to be at Gizah the palm-tree under which the Blessed Virgin suckled Jesus, and this palm-tree was said to have been

40

the only one in the region which bore any fruit. On their way southward, they would have seen the site on the bank of the Nile where Moses was hid in an ark of bulrushes and where he was discovered by Pharaoh's daughter (*Ex.* 2:3-5). Maqrizi states that the ark in which Moses was hid at the banks of the Nile is kept at the Mosque of Tubah at Gizah.

Some twelve kilometres south of Cairo, at Ma'adi on the very bank of the Nile, there is the Church of the Blessed Virgin with its three cupolas. Here, according to an oral tradition, there was at the time of the Holy Family's visit a synagogue which the Holy Family attended. Joseph became acquainted with the sailors of the Nile boats, and the Holy Family was invited to be taken south to Upper Egypt. One of the monks of the Dair al-Muharraq (The Monastery of the Blessed Virgin) added that the Holy Family was able to afford these rather extensive travels because of the treasure, the gold, frankincense and myrrh which had been presented to the Christ child by the wise men from the East (*Matth.* 2:11). To this day, the flight of stairs leading from the churchyard to the Nile marks the site where the Holy Family embarked on their journey southwards.

In addition to this oral tradition of the Holy Family's visit to Ma'adi, Abu 'l-Makarim, incorrectly called Abu Salih, speaks of the Church of the Pure Lady Mary, called al-Martuti, which was surmounted by a cupola. According to this thirteenth-century writer, this particular site was in ancient days a place of worship of the Israelites when they were in bondage in Egypt; and when the Holy Family came down into Egypt, they sat in this place, where there is now a picture of the Blessed Virgin before the holy altar. The church was founded by the Copts under the name of the Lady, and was called al-Martuti, which is from the Greek words Meter Theou (Mother of God). According to al-Idrisi, the Church of al-Martuti was situated in Munyat as-Sudan, on the western (*sic*) bank of the Nile, about twenty-five kilometres south of Cairo. This would place the locality in question south of Badreshein.

41

Maqrizi, the Muslim historian of the fifteenth century, mentions a palm-tree in Ahnassiah al-Madinat, the ancient city of Herakleopolis in the Province of Beni Suef, which was seen there until the end of the 'Ummayad Dynasty (750 A.D.). This palm tree is supposed to have been the one of which the Quran speaks: "And the pangs of childbirth drove her (the Blessed Virgin) unto the trunk of the palm tree. She said: 'O, would that I had died ere this, and had become a thing of naught, forgotten'. Then (one) cried unto her from below her, saying: 'Grieve not, thy Lord has placed a rivulet beneath thee. And shake the trunk of the palm tree toward thee, thou wilt cause ripe dates to fall upon thee'." (XIX, 23-25) Passing through the Nile Valley, the Holy Family must have crossed several times the many irrigation canals which were constructed during the Roman occupation by the *epistrategoi* of Middle Egypt. These canals, we are told, were full of crocodiles, which in Arsinoe (Fayum), the ancient Crocodilopolis, were even accounted sacred.

Situated twelve kilometres south-west of Maghaghah is the small village of Ishnin an-Nassarah. A local oral tradition relates that the water of the well, about eighty metres north of the Church of St. George, was blessed by Jesus when the Holy Family passed through this village on their way to where later Dair al-Ganus was built. Another version of this local tradition speaks of a well under the baptistry at the western end of the southern aisle of the church. In former times, many people offered prayers in Ishnin, so that there were as many churches in this locality as there were days in the year.

In the *Ethiopic Synaxarium* it is stated that the Holy Family went to a locality which is called Baysus (Bet Iyasus) and here Jesus dug a well whereof the water cured every sickness and every pain. And He also set a sign in a certain river of Egypt, which rose in flood every year. At the time of prayer at which they offered up incense at midday to God by that well, as soon as the reading of the Gospel was ended, the water which was in the well would rise up and come to the mouth of the well, and they used to receive a blessing from it, and straightway the water would recede until it reached its former level, and the people used to measure by the cubit the height to which it rose above its normal level at the bottom of the well. If the height were twenty cubits, there would be great abundance in the land of Egypt, if the height were eighteen or seventeen cubits, there would also be abundance, but if the height were only sixteen cubits, there would be a great famine throughout the land of Egypt. Maqrizi adds to the tradition by saying that this well was situated in the church of the Monastery of Arjanus, and that on the night of the 25th of Bashons (June 2nd), the people would assemble to remove the stone cover from the well, when they would discover that the water within had risen and begun to sink again.

The fact that an older church existed at this site is testified by M. de Maillet (1703), French consul general, who developed a keen interest in all things pertaining to Egypt. He mentions a village called by the Arabs Bir el-Gernous, and states that in this place the Copts have a sacred well, by which they foretell the height of the annual inundation. With an elaborate ritual, a cotton cord marked at regular intervals by threads of white and blue is let down into the well, so that the end touches the water. Then a table is placed over the mouth of the well, and the bishop celebrates the Divine Liturgy. When the Liturgy is finished, the table is taken away and the cord is examined. According to Coptic belief, the height to which the water has penetrated the cord marks the height to which the water will rise.

Doubtless we have here a reference to an ancient Nilometer. There were Nilometers also at Philae, Edfu, Esnah, Luxor, Memphis and the Island of Roda (Cairo) by which the government calculated the annual revenue. Apart from the above mentioned sources, I have not found any further reference to a Nilometer at this locality.

The site of Baysus is now the village of Dair al-Ganus, about seven kilometres west of Ishnin an Nassarah, and eighteen kilometres south-west of Maghaghah. Here it should be pointed out that the village of al-Ganus should not be confused with the village of Dair al-Ganus, where to this day the sacred well is to be found. The well from which according to local tradition the Holy Family drank, is situated at the western end of the south aisle of the Church of the Blessed Virgin. This church was built in about 1870.

In commemoration of the blessings which this village received through the visit of the Holy Family, the people celebrate annually a fair (*mulid*) on the 15th and 16th of Misra (August 21st and 22nd), during which time the pilgrims are said to be never bitten by vermin, while the children even play with scorpions. The number of pilgrims who attend this fair varies between 5000 to 6000 people, who use the water of the well for drinking purposes.

Ten kilometres in a southerly direction, there is situated on the edge of the desert the ancient city of Oxyrhynchus, in Coptic Pemje, the present town of al-Bahnasa, a city which in ancient times was the capital of a nome. In Pharaonic times the fish Oxyrhynchus, a species of mormyrus, was worshipped here. Plutarch relates that the people of the neighbouring town of Cynopolis used to venerate the dog, and how a quarrel arose between the two towns because the citizens of the one had killed and fed on the sacred animal of the other.

According to Maqrizi, the Copts are in agreement that the Holy Family visited al-Bahnasa, and a commentator of the Quran mentions that the passage "and we have made the Son of Mary and His Mother a portent, and we gave them refuge on a height, a place of flocks and water-springs," (*XXIII*, 50) refers to al-Bahnasa. Another Muslim tradition relates that the Holy Family travelled on an ass to al-Bahnasa, where there was a well in the chapel from which one could receive healing from infirmities. It was here, where the Blessed Virgin and her Son washed before prayer, that all the water spilled over and then disappeared. Another commentator adds that at the time of their arrival at al-Bahnasa, the Holy Family went to the place of the famous well, and that Joseph returned, leaving the Blessed Virgin near the well. Then Jesus asked for water, and He began to weep because of His thirst, and there was no water at that time, but the level of the water rose so that Jesus could drink, and since that day the Christians have celebrated this event.

Muhammad al-Baqir (676-731 A.D.) says that when Jesus was nine months old, His Mother took Him to the school in al-Bahnasa. The teacher said to Jesus: "Say the alphabet." Jesus lifted up His head and said: "Dost thou know what these words mean?" The teacher wished to strike Him, but Jesus said: "Do not strike me, but if thou dost not know, ask me and I shall explain to thee." "Speak," said the teacher. "Come down from thy desk," answered Jesus. The teacher came down and Jesus took his place and began to say: "The *Alif* stands for the good deeds of God, the *Da* for the glory of God, the *Gim* for the splendour of God, the *Dal* for the religion of God, the *Ha* for the abyss of Hell, the *Wa* indicates the misery of those living in Hell, the *Ha* means the remission of sins of those who ask for forgiveness, the *K* is the word of God which will never change, the *Sad* is the measure for a measure, the *Ta* stands for the serpents of hell." "Well," said the teacher to the Blessed Virgin, "take thy Son and watch over Him, for God hath given to Him wisdom and He doth not need a teacher." This tradition should be compared with the almost identical story in the *Gospel of Thomas the Israelite* (140-160 A.D.).

Wahb (d. 728 A.D.) relates that the Holy Family stayed at a hospice for the poor at al-Bahnasa, which was supported by a *diqhan,* a nobleman of the king. One day, an important part of the diqhan's treasure was stolen, and the Blessed Virgin was afflicted about the misfortune. When Jesus realized His Mother's distress, He said to her: "Mother, dost thou wish me to show where the diqhan's money is?" The Blessed Virgin

The infant Jesus teaching the true nature of the alphabet

informed the diqhan of what Jesus had said. When they were all gathered together, Jesus approached two men, one of whom was blind and the other lame, the latter being carried by the blind man. Then Jesus said to the blind man: "Arise!" "This I cannot do," said the blind man. "How then was it possible for you to steal?" When they heard this, they struck the blind man until he showed Jesus where the treasure was. This then was their trick. The blind man used his strength and the lame man his eyes. The stolen treasure was restored to the diqhan.

Oxyrhynchus (al-Bahnasa) used to be an episcopal see, and in the fifth century it is said to have possessed 10,000 monks and 12,000 nuns. Among the many famous Christians who have come from Oxyrhynchus, there is Dermataus, an ascete and founder of a monastery, and Harman, Bishop of Qaou in Upper Egypt. There is evidence that the persecutions by the Emperor Diocletian were especially severe at Oxyrhynchus. Elias the Eunuch, Isaac of Tiphre and Epiuse suffered martyrdom here.

In 1897 B.P. Grenfell and A.S. Hunt, whilst excavating, discovered in the mounds of Oxyrhynchus the famous *Logia* or *Sayings of Jesus,* which form part of the find known as the Oxyrhynchus Papyri. Today, al-Bahnasa possesses only one church and this is dedicated to St. George and was built in 1923. The Christians of al-Bahnasa believe that the Holy Family stayed on the west bank of the Bahr Yusuf Canal, which strictly speaking is an arm of the Nile, though there are no traces left which would indicate their visit.

Near the ancient Cynopolis, the present village of al-Kais, the Holy Family embarked on a boat to travel southwards. After thirty-five kilometres they passed the Gabal at-Tair, which is almost opposite to Samalut and Bihu. Abu 'l-Makarim recalls that, when the Holy Family passed this mountain, a large rock threatened to fall upon the boat, and the Blessed Virgin was very frightened. Jesus, however, extended His hand and prevented the rock from falling, and the imprint of His hand remained on the rock. In the imprint of His hand there is a fine perforation, large enough to admit a collyrium needle, into which the needle is inserted and, when it is pulled out, brings upon it a black collyrium which makes an indelible mark. It is said however that when Almeric, King of Jerusalem (1162-1173 A.D.) invaded Upper Egypt to drive out Shirkuh the Kurd and his men from Egypt, they cut away the piece of rock upon which was the mark of the palm of the hand, and took it back with them to Syria in 1168.

In order to visit the famous Church of the Blessed Virgin at Gabal at-Tair, it is advisable to take a sailing boat either from Minya or from Samalut, since there is no road on the east bank of the Nile. Alternatively, one can cross the Nile by boat from Bihu, twenty kilometres north of Minya, though one should allow at least two hours for the crossing, as it depends on the wind. Having reached the east bank of the Nile, one climbs the 166 steps cut in the face of the cliff and reaches the church which is reputed to have been built by St. Helena, the mother of St. Constantine. A memorial tablet on the west wall of the nave states that the first church was built in 44 A.M. or 328 A.D., and that it was repaired by Anba Sawirus, Metropolitan of Minya, in 1938. To this day, the Church of the Blessed Virgin attracts annually up to 10,000 visitors who come by sailing boats from as far as Assiut, and even from Cairo.

From Gabal at-Tair the Holy Family sailed southwards, passing on their way first the port of Khoufou, the present Minya, then the rock temple of the goddess Pekhet, called by the Greeks Speos Artemides, on the site of which is the present village of Beni Hassan ash-Shuruk, and finally, the temple of Ramses II, on the ruins of which the Roman Emperor Hadrian built in 130 A.D. the town of Antinoupolis. The site is occupied by the present village of the Shaikh 'Abadah.

Opposite the ruins of Antinoupolis there is the town of al-Rodah, which is built on the site where the Holy Family disembarked in order to proceed to the famous city of

Khmunu, the Hermopolis Magna of the Greeks, at present, the village of al-Ashmunain.

In their travels, the Holy Family took advantage of the natural means of communication by water along the Nile, and where this or a side-canal was not available, donkeys or camels were used. Generally speaking, during the latter period of the reign of Augustus, Egypt remained in a state of comparative tranquility. At the same time, the Romans collected a large number of various taxes which became a real burden for the Egyptians. The receipts of tolls paid by travellers give abundant evidence of this important means of gathering revenue. Strabo mentions that tolls were collected at Hermopolis which was the nearest town to the dividing line between the Thebaid and Middle Egypt. In most cases an *ad valorem* duty was collected, which in Upper Egypt consisted of two percent on the goods or commodities. Thus, the Holy Family was taxed at least once during their travels to Upper Egypt.

According to the *Vision of Theophilus,* the Holy Family found images of horses at all four corners of the gate which led into Hermopolis Magna. These, however, fell down and were broken when the Holy Family entered the city. *The Book of the Bee,* on the other hand, states that there were by the two buttresses of the gate two figures of brass which had been made by the sages and philosophers. And when the Holy Family passed through the gate, these two figures cried out with a loud voice saying: "A great king has come into Egypt!" *The Gospel of Pseudo-Matthew,* which also attests the visit of the Holy Family to Hermopolis Magna, mentions that Aphrodosius, the governor of the city, when he saw that the idols were destroyed, adored the Child and said to those present: "Unless this were the God of our gods, they would not have fallen. If we do not adore Him, as they have done, we are in danger of such destruction as fell upon Pharaoh who was drowned with his army." When the king of Egypt, however, heard this, he was troubled and moved, for he feared lest his

49

kingdom should be taken away from him. And he commanded the heralds to proclaim throughout the whole city: "If a man knoweth, let him point Him out to us without delay." And when they had made such a search, and did not find Him, the king commanded all the inhabitants of the city to go outside and to come in one by one. When Jesus entered, the two figures of brass cried out: "This is the king!" And when Jesus was revealed, the king sought to slay Him. Now Lazarus, whom Jesus raised from the dead, was there, and was one of the king's officials, and he was held in much esteem by the king. He drew near to Joseph and asked them: "Whence are ye?" They said to him: "From the land of Palestine." When he heard that they were from Palestine, he was sorry for them and went to the king and pledged himself for the Child. This then is the cause of the love between Lazarus and Jesus. The *Ethiopic Synaxarium* states that the Holy Family dwelt here with a man called Apelon, whereas the *Coptic Synaxarium* calls the host Taloun.

There was a tree in Hermopolis Magna which worshipped the traces of the steps of Jesus, and Jesus said unto the tree: "Let no worm be found in thee for ever, but be thou a remembrance to all of my entry into this town," and He touched the Mukantah tree. The Byzantine historian Sozomen (*Hist. Eccl.* V, 21) calls this tree Persea.

After this, five camels came near the Holy Family and they began to walk in the market, and they rendered the road too narrow, and Jesus looked at them, and in that hour they became stones. This detail may have been suggested by an avenue of sphinxes at al-Ashmunain, such as is found at Luxor.

On the following day, great multitudes of sick people assembled around Jesus, and Jesus laid His hand on each of them and healed them of their infirmities.

Abu 'l-Makarim adds further that the Church of the Blessed Virgin at al-Ashmunain contained several altars and marble pillars. One altar was used for the celebration of the Divine

Liturgy all the time, for upon it was the mark of the hand of the Lord. Outside the church was a Syrian tree which bore the fruit called Sebastan, which is of red colour. This is the tree which bowed its head when Jesus approached it. The governor of the town wished to cut down this tree, but Agathus, the thirty-ninth Patriarch of Alexandria (658-677 A.D.), was standing under the tree, and when the wood-cutter struck it with his axe, the axe flew back into his face. Thereupon the governor never again gave orders to cut down the tree.

Today there is no trace left of the Holy Family's visit to al-Ashmunain, and there is not now even a Coptic church in this once famous Christian city. About ten kilometres southwards, the Holy Family stayed for a few days in Manlau, the present town of Mallawi. There are numerous Coptic churches in this town; among others, one is dedicated to St. Mercurius, one to St. George, and two to the Blessed Virgin.

Two days further travelling in a southerly direction brought the Holy Family to the town of Kenis, (Nikyas, Funkus) the present Dairut as-Sharif. The inhabitants of this town were very charitable, and the Holy Family remained there for several days, and Jesus wrought innumerable miracles in that place, and all those who had diseases or afflictions came to Him with faith to be healed. After this, Dianos, a carpenter who had known Joseph in Jerusalem, invited the Holy Family to stay with him. He had a son who was possessed of a devil, and when Jesus came near unto him, the devil took the boy and dashed him to the ground and cried out: "What have I to do with Thee, O Jesus of Nazareth? We left Jerusalem to Thee and came to this town, and Thou followest us to torment us. Verily, Thou art the Son of God." Then Jesus said: "O accursed devil, shut up thy mouth and come out of him." And the child was healed in that very hour, and many people believed in Him. After Jesus had performed these miracles, the idols in the town were broken up and smashed to pieces.

From Dairut as-Sharif, the Holy Family travelled via

Pepleu, the present Beblaw, to the town of Sanabu. At one time, Sanabu was an episcopal see, but already in the fifteenth century the monastery at Sanabu was deserted.

According to the *I Infancy Gospel,* the Holy Family always received sufficient provision for their journey from the people who received them. Once, when they entered a certain town, there was a marriage which was then about to be performed. The arts of Satan and the practices of the sorcerers, however, caused the bride to be dumb, so that she could not so much as open her mouth. But when this dumb bride saw the Blessed Virgin entering into the town, and carrying the Child in her arms, she stretched out her hands to Jesus and took Him into her arms, and closely hugging Him, she kissed Him repeatedly, and straightway the string of her tongue was loosened, and her ears were opened and she began to sing praises unto God who had restored her speech and hearing.

Thereupon, the Holy Family entered the city of Cusae or Kuskam, nowadays the village of al-Qusia where, according to Aelianus, Venus Urania and her cow were worshipped. As the ancient city of Gosu it had served as the capital of the Lower Sycamore Nome. At the time of the Holy Family's visit there was a temple of idols which was surmounted by an idol on which there were seven veils. When Jesus reached the gate of Cusae, the seven veils were rent asunder, and the idol fell to the ground and was dashed to pieces. Then the devils who were in the idol threatened the priests and cried: "If thou dost not pursue that woman and the Child who is with her, and the old man who is with them, and the other woman, namely Salome, and drive them away,and if thou let them enter this town, they will put an end to thy service, and we will leave the town." When the priests of the idols, who were a hundred in number, heard this speech of the idols, they pursued the Holy Family with rods and axes in order to strike them. Thereupon the Holy Family left the town, and after they had travelled a little distance, Jesus turned and cursed the town, saying: "Let its people be in an estate lower than that of all other people, and let them be more lowly and suppressed than all the inhabitants of the Land of Egypt. Let its earth be cursed, so that nothing shall grow in it except halfa and rush-nut."

Today, al-Qusia is an insignificant village except for its railway-station which is used annually by thousands of pilgrims to the fair (*mulid*) which is held in commemoration of the first Church of the Blessed Virgin at Philippi (June 20th) at the Dair al-Muharraq.

After Jesus had cursed the town of Cusae and its inhabitants, the Holy Family went on a short distance south (actually six kilometres west) of the town, and they rested for a while in a certain locality on account of their weariness and fatigue. Here, in the present village of Meir, Jesus took the olive wood staff of Joseph and planted it in the ground and said: "Thou shalt serve as a testimony of My arrival here." And immediately the staff took root and began to blossom.

Then in the evening the Holy Family went up to a mountain, probably up to those hills situated one kilometre west of Meir, and lo, the two brigands whom the Holy Family had met at Basatah (Tell al-Bastah) came towards them. They had followed them from one place to another, and when they saw the Holy Family in this deserted mountain, they approached them with drawn daggers, unsheathed swords and their faces masked and said: "Ye have exhausted us, because we have pursued you for many days and have not found you, and have not had an opportunity to meet with you so as to plunder you, except at this moment, when ye have fallen into our hands. Today, we will strip you of your garments and rob you." And they snatched Jesus from the arm of His Mother and stripped Him of His garments. Then they took the garments of the Blessed Virgin, and they even took her veil. Then they stripped also Joseph, who was standing by speechless as a lamb. As for Salome, when she perceived what was taking place, she threw her garments to them before they came to her.

After they had taken the garments, the brigands went away a short distance, and the Blessed Virgin who was greatly perturbed said within herself: "Perchance they will return and kill my Son. Would that I were in Bethlehem, because then they would have recognized the old Joseph who would have implored them not to kill my Son. Would that they would kill me before killing my Son, that I may not see His great affliction. If they were to kill my Son, I would kill myself with my own hands."

While the Blessed Virgin was uttering these words and lamenting and weeping, her tears streamed down her cheeks. Then one of the brigands looked towards her and saw her weeping, and his nerves were shaken, and he spoke to his companion who was a Jew, a Syrian, and said to him: "O my companion, I beseech thee today not to take the garments of these strangers, because I perceive on their faces a light greater than that on all the faces of mankind. This child resembles a prince, the like of whom I have never seen." The Jewish brigand said to the Egyptian brigand: "I will not listen to thee this time, as I wish to take their garments, because they are royal garments which will bring us much wealth for our living." Then the Egyptian brigand asked for his portion of the garments that it should be given to him, for he was much distressed at the nakedness of the Holy Family, and he returned his portion of the garments to them. When Jesus had put on His garments, He looked at the brigand and stretched out His finger and made the sign of the Cross over Him. Then the two brigands proceeded on their way, and Jesus said to His Mother: "O Mary, the Jews will crucify Me in Jerusalem. And these two brigands whom thou seest, one of them will be crucified on my right hand, and the other on my left hand. The Egyptian will be crucified on my right hand, and the Jew on my left, and the brigand who hath returned our garments will confess Me and believe in Me on the Cross, and he will be the first to enter Paradise, even before Adam and all his descendants."

The story of the two brigands

And all sick persons who shall come in future to the place where the brigands stripped Jesus, and shall be stripped of their garments and be bathed, Jesus will heal them in honour of the fact that there He was stripped of His garments.

Not far away, about eight kilometres south of Meir, the Holy Family discovered a well, though it was dried up. However, when the Blessed Virgin took Jesus to the well and He stretched forth His finger and blessed it, it became full. While searching around, Salome came upon a wash-basin and a water jug, as if they had been placed there purposely for them. It was always Salome who bathed Jesus and His Mother who gave Him milk. And often while her nipples were in the mouth of Jesus, she saw the angels and celestial beings prostrating themselves and worshipping Jesus.

Satan, however, appeared to Herod and said to him: "Thou slewest the innocent children of Bethlehem in order to find Mary and her Son, and thou didst not find them. I shall tell thee now where they are; the woman and her Son are hidden in a desert place on the southern side of the land of Egypt. Arise and dispatch ten of thy soldiers to repair to that place and to kill them, and thus thou wilt be confirmed in thy kingdom. If thou dost not listen to me and dost not do what I tell thee, then tomorrow this Child will grow up and go to Jerusalem, both He and His Mother, and He will perform numerous and great miracles there. When thy soldiers depart to inquire after them, let them proceed as far as Cusae (Kuskam), and then let them travel to the west side of it, as far as the mountain, until they find them in the place, where they are living alone, for they have sought in all the land of Egypt and not found anybody who would offer them shelter." Thereupon, Herod assembled all the chiefs and elders and told them what had taken place and they said: "O our Lord, let it be as thou desirest." And Herod chose ten valiant men and he informed them of the place in which the Holy Family were to be found, and he said to them: "When ye have found them, bring them unto me that

I may kill them with my own hands. If ye do what I have commanded you, I will give unto each of you ten talents of gold, and ye shall be great in all my kingdom." And the soldiers mounted their steeds in order to pursue the Holy Family.

Now there was a man from the children of Israel, of the tribe of Judah and the family of the kings, who was related to Joseph, and his name was Moses. When he heard this news, he went unto Joseph with great speed and Divine help, and he came unto the Holy Family within three days, for he travelled in the night more than in the day. When Joseph saw Moses, he recognized him, and he rose up to greet him. And Moses told him what had taken place, and of what Herod had done, and how he had killed the children of Bethlehem and Jerusalem, and how he had searched for the Divine Child. When the Blessed Virgin heard all this, she was exceedingly sorrowful and she trembled with fear, but Jesus comforted her, and they turned to Moses, and Jesus said unto him: "Thou hast come unto us in order that thou mayest inform us of this thing. Thy coming and thy labour shall of a truth be rewarded, but because of the fear which thou hast caused to My Mother, take hold of this stone on which I was bathed, and put it beneath thy head, and sleep and rest for a little while." And he took the stone and placed it beneath his head, and turning his face toward the east, he gave up the ghost. Joseph took his body and buried it in this house under the threshold, towards the interior. And his memory survives till this day. Thus the spirit of Moses became a guardian of the house against the intrusion of evil spirits.

After this, the Holy Family sojourned for six months in this house. Then Jesus said to His Mother: "This house in which we are shall contain holy monks on whom no rule in this world shall be able to inflict any injury, because it has been a refuge to us. Any barren woman who beseecheth Me with a pure heart and calleth to mind this house, unto her will I give sons.

There shall, moreover, be in this place a blessed congregation who shall remember and bless My Name, and pray unto Me at all times, and so gain strength against all their adversaries. Those women in travail who shall be mindful of Me and of the labour which thou didst endure with Me, their prayers will I hear, and they shall be relieved."

This holy place, blessed on account of the Holy Family's presence in it, was dedicated to the Blessed Virgin and is known as the Dair al-Muharraq. Pilgrimages to this church have been made by multitudes of people from all districts of Egypt from ancient times to the present day, by reason of the signs and wonders which have been manifested here.

Abu 'l-Makarim states that the Holy Family stayed in a chamber on the upper storey of the church, which is reached by mounting a flight of steps. In this chamber there is a window which was opened by the breath of Jesus, for it was not opened by the hand of man nor by any tool.

According to tradition, the Church of the Blessed Virgin at the Dair al-Muharraq was the first church built in Egypt, and the monks believe that this church was built immediately after St. Mark's arrival in Egypt, sometime about 60 A.D. The present church may be assigned to the twelfth or thirteenth century. It lies about 1.20 metres below the present ground-level of the inner court of the monastery, and it is used for the daily celebration of the Divine Liturgy.

The Dair al-Muharraq belongs to that group of monasteries which were established by St. Pachomius, or Anba Bakhum as he is called in Arabic, (d. 349 A.D.) or by his immediate successors. Of its sixteen hundred years of history almost nothing is known, except for the fact that four patriarchs of the see of Alexandria came from there. Since the nineteenth century, this monastery has been known for its wealth and the charitable work which it performs among the peasants of the Nile Valley.

An oral tradition in Assiut asserts that the most southern

place visited by the Holy Family in Egypt was ten kilometres south-west of Assiut, the ancient Lycopolis or "wolf town". To this day, about 80,000 pilgrims assemble annually at the foot of Istabl 'Antar (Antar's stable), a mountain range rising west of Assiut, to commemorate and celebrate the stay of the Holy Family in the large rock-tombs of the Ninth to the Twelfth Dynasty.

The fact that the above mentioned site has had a long Christian tradition cannot be denied, since Maqrizi lists numerous monasteries and churches which were situated here. In times of persecution, pious believers took refuge in the caves of this ancient necropolis to live a life of penitence apart from the world. One of these, John of Lycopolis (fourth century), bore the reputation of a saint and even a prophet. Yet the oral tradition, which is upheld by hundreds of thousands of Copts and which is supported by Anba Mikhail, Bishop of Assiut, that a first century church was built here in commemoration of the stay of the Holy Family, cannot be verified.

The Church of the Blessed Virgin at Dair al-Adhra was built by Anba Mikhail in 1955. The church is situated east of the cave in which the Holy Family supposedly rested. The episcopal residence is situated north of the church, and the present building activities lead one to believe that this annual feast which is held between August 7th and August 22nd will eventually become the largest Christian *mulid* in Egypt.

From Assiut, so the oral tradition continues, the Holy Family returned to the site of the present Dair al-Muharraq.

3
The Return of the Holy Family to Palestine

And it came to pass that during their sojourn at the place where there is now the Dair al-Muharraq, while Joseph was sleeping, the angel of the Lord appeared unto him in a dream and said: "Arise and take the young child and his mother, and go into the land of Israel, for they are dead which sought the young child's life." (*Matth.* 2:20) Obeying the voice of the angel, the Holy Family thereupon returned to Palestine. Having left Cusae, they came again to the town of Hermopolis Magna (al-Ashmunain), and we read in the *Vision of Theophilus,* that its inhabitants received them with great joy and jubilation. The present village of al-Ashmunain is situated near the famous city of Khmunu, which was the chief place of worship of Tut, the god of writing and of science. Furthermore, it was also the capital of the Hare Nome of Upper Egypt. Fr. Claude Sicard, who visited this town in 1716, wrote to the Count of Toulouse that it contained the remains of a large number of palaces, of marble and granite columns, all of which pointed to its former splendour. Recent excavations at the "Great City of Hermes" as carried out by Dr. Sami Gabra, substantiate that the site of Hermopolis Magna was one of the most important cities in ancient Egyptian history.

A local oral tradition in the village of Dair al-Barsha, on the east bank of the Nile opposite Mallawi, states that the Holy Family visited the village and stayed for some time in a cave nearby. The Magharat al-Adhra, the Cave of the Holy Virgin, is situated in the mountains east of Dair al-Barsha. Normally, the cave is locked with an iron door, and those interested in visiting it ought to obtain the key from the Coptic priest either in Dair al-Barsha or in Dair Abu Hinnis. On the east wall of the cave, there is a painting on plaster showing the Holy Virgin seated on a chair and knitting. Moreover there is a carpenter's bench and a plane, objects which according to tradition were used by St. Joseph. Every year, on the occasion of the Feast of St. Bishoi on July 15th, people visit the cave in commemoration of the visit and stay of the Holy Family in Dair al-Barsha.

There is good reason to believe that the Holy Family returned to Palestine by the same way they had come. According to the *Coptic Synaxarium,* on their return the Holy Family lodged in a cave which to-day is situated beneath the Church of St. Sergius (Abu Sargah) in Old Cairo, the ancient Babylon of Egypt. Supposedly this church was built during the patriarchate of John II (505-516 A.D.).

It is quite likely that the Holy Family stayed for some time at Babylon, where since the days of the Exile (597-538 B.C.) Jews had lived. The present Synagogue of Abraham Ben Ezra (ca. 1150 A.D.), the former Coptic Church of St. Michael, was built on the site of an ancient synagogue where, according to Jewish tradition, Jeremiah had preached. No doubt the Holy Family would have been attracted to stay with their countrymen, especially since they had lived for three years in an environment which, culturally speaking, must have appeared to them so alien. An oral tradition states that Joseph met with some members of his family at Babylon who persuaded him to spend some time with them.

Babylon, according to Strabo, was a strong fortress, and as mentioned above, one of the three legions stationed in Egypt was encamped here. A mountainous ridge extended from the encampment as far as the Nile. At this ridge, the Holy Family must have seen the wheels and screws by which water was raised from the river. One hundred and fifty prisoners were employed in the operation of this aqueduct. It should be remembered, however, that since the construction of the fortress, the Nile has changed its course, which means that the Nile flows now some four hundred metres farther west than it did then. The present ruins of Babylon near the Coptic Museum in Old Cairo, however, are the remains of second-century fortifications. Trajan (98-117 A.D.) had replaced the older encampment which was situated on higher ground in order to obtain better water supply and river communication.

The tradition of their visit to Babylon is well attested by the Synaxaria and the reports of the pilgrims. When the pilgrim of Placentia, known as Antoninus Martyr (560-570 A.D.) passed through Egypt, he saw at Memphis (sic) a temple, which is now a church, a door of which had closed of its own accord before our Lord when He was there with the Blessed Virgin, and it could not be opened. "There he saw a linen cloth, upon which was a portrait of the Saviour, Who, as the people said, wiped His face upon it, and His image remained there. This image is adored at certain times, and we adored it, but because of its brightness we were not able to look fixedly upon it, because the more earnestly you fix your gaze upon it, the more it changes before your eyes." The fact that our pilgrim speaks of Memphis does not necessarily exclude the probability that his report really refers to Babylon, for it is well known that Arab writers often transferred the name of Memphis to Misr al-Kadimah. They imagined, indeed, that the city of Memphis had occupied the site of Babylon. Furthermore, Alfred Butler points out that at the time of Diocletian, the city names of Memphis and Babylon were used interchangeably.

For the mediaeval pilgrims to the Holy Land, the Cave of the Holy Family was a site which was included in their itineraries. John Poloner (1421) went out of his way to visit the underground chapel, where he saw a cross which had been made over the place where the Babe had slept. At the time of his visit, the church was called the Church of Our Lady of Cana in Babylon. Felix Fabri (1483) refers to the church which was dedicated to the Blessed Virgin, where they took out their processionals and made a tour of the building, visiting the crypt, and noticing near the altar in the upper church a great deep hole, like a big tomb, full of water, from which they were told Joseph drew water for washing the Divine Child. That Western Christians also accepted this tradition is confirmed by the fact that until the eighteenth century the Franciscan Friars used to celebrate the Holy Mass on the altar in the crypt.

The crypt is situated beneath the centre of the choir and part of the central sanctuary of the Church of St. Sergius. It is entered by two stairways which lead down from the northern and southern sanctuaries. During the inundation of the Nile, this crypt is flooded for about two months. By its contact with this sacred spot this water is considered holy and is much resorted to by the faithful.

From Babylon the Holy Family continued their way northwards, stopping again at On, near the site of the present village of Matariyah. Here they bathed, and the well was blessed thereby. Today Matariyah is a townlet which can be reached from Cairo by bus or train. The sycamore tree stands in a small garden enclosed by a wall on the right-hand side of the main street coming from Cairo, just before the Catholic Church of Our Lady of Matariyah.

The next place which the Holy Family is said to have visited on their return to Palestine was al-Mahammah, or the place of bathing. In ancient times, a temple with many idols stood there, which however collapsed and broke into pieces when the Holy Family came near. According to the *Coptic Synaxarium,* a source of water commemorates the place where the Holy Family bathed.

We should remember that the practice of frequent lustrations, partial or entire, was enjoined on all Jews by the Law, while on the other hand, the Graeco-Roman habit of bathing the entire body must have penetrated far down through the social strata of the day. This would explain, at least to some extent, the emphasis laid upon springs and wells as stopping places for the Holy Family.

In the Church of the Blessed Virgin at Musturud, about three kilometres west of Matariyah, on the western bank of the Ismailiyah Canal, there is to this day a well which was blessed by the Holy Family. The well is situated in the north east corner of the church, east of the cave, where the Holy Family found shelter. Stairs from the east and the west lead down to the cave to which thousands of people come for the annual fair (mulid) which is held between August 7th and 22nd.

From al-Mahammah, the next halting-place of the Holy Family was Leontopolis, known today as the ruins of Tell al-Yehudiyah and referred to in old Roman maps as Vicus Judaeorum. An oral tradition of the Christians of Shibin al-Kanatir (two kilometres north-west of the ancient Leontopolis) states that the Holy Family visited their countrymen who had settled around the Temple of Onias. The high priest Onias IV went to Egypt in 154 B.C. to seek aid against the tyranny of the Seleucids at the court of the Ptolemies who were their political enemies. With the permission of Ptolemy IV (Philometer) he built at Leontopolis a temple which, though comparatively small, was modeled on that of Jerusalem. This town was so important that after the destruction of Heliopolis, it became the capital of the Nome of Heliopolis.

Onias doubtless expected that after the desecration of the

Temple in Jerusalem by Antiochus Epiphanes (170 B.C.), the Egyptian temple would be regarded as the only legitimate one, but the traditional teachings of Judaism as contained in the Mishnah concede only quasi-legitimate status to the temple of Onias, in fact even for the Egyptian Jews the latter did not possess the same importance as did the Temple in Jerusalem. Today most of the ruins are buried in rubbish.

From Tell al-Yehudiyah, the Holy Family returned to Palestine the way they had come to Egypt, passing through Bilbais, the Wadi Tumilat, the isthmus at al-Qantara, and then travelling on the caravan route from Egypt to Palestine along the Mediterranean coast. According to a local tradition, the Holy Family rested for several days near Gaza. In a garden between the Gabal Muntar and Gaza, the Christians of Gaza point out the place where the Holy Family stayed on their return.

Generally speaking, the Holy Family would have stayed with people whose acquaintance they had made during their travels in Egypt, except, of course, where they chose to journey by a different route. *The Infancy Gospel of St. Thomas* records that the three year-old Jesus joined one day some boys who were playing. He took a dried fish and put it into a basin and commanded it to move to and fro, and it began to move. Then He said to the fish: "Cast out the salt which is in thee and go into the water," and it came to pass. But when the neighbours saw what was done, they told it to the widow in whose house His Mother dwelt. And she, when she heard it, hastened and cast them out of her house.

When the Holy Family entered Palestine, Joseph heard "that Archaelaus did reign in Judaea in the room of his father Herod, he was afraid to go thither, notwithstanding, being warned of God in a dream, he turned aside into the parts of Galilee, and he came and dwelt in a city called Nazareth, that it might be fulfilled which was spoken by the prophets, He shall be called a Nazarene." (*Matt* 2:22-23).

Bibliography and Acknowledgments

Chapter 1

Appian, *De Bello Civili.* (Bohn's Classical Libr., 1899).

Caesar, Julius, *De Bello Civili.* (De Pontet, Oxford Classical Texts, 1900).

Cicero, *Ad Atticum.* (Muller, Oxford Classical Texts. 1880-96).

Eutropius, *Breviarum ab urbe condita.* (Pirogoff, *De Eutropii breviarii,* 1873).

Hirtius, *Bellum Alexandrinum.* (Seel, "Hirtius", *Klio,* Beiheft, 1935).

Josephus, Flavius, *Antiquities of the Jews.* (Whiston, *The Works,* I).

Lucanus, *De Bello Civili.* (Ed. Housman, Oxford, 1926).

Plutarch, *Vit. Anton., Vit. Pomp., Vit. J. Caes.* (*The Lives of the Noble Grecians and Romans,* Great Books of the Western World, XIV).

Strabo, *The Geography.* (Bohn's Classical Libr., 1857).

Tacitus, *The Annals.* (Great Books of the Western Western World, XV).

Bell, Idris, *Egypt from Alexander the Great to the Arab Conquest.* Oxford, 1940.

Cantarelli, L., *La Serie dei prefetti di Egitto.* Rome, 1906-13.

Lesquier, J., *L'armée Romaine d'Egypte d'Auguste à Dioclétian.* Cairo, 1918.

Milne, J.G., *A History of Egypt under Roman Rule.* London, 1924.

Schubart, W., *Aegypten von Alexander dem Grossen bis auf Mohammed,* Berlin, 1922.

Sharpe, S., *The History of Egypt, II,* London, 1870.

Stein, A., *Untersuchungen zur Geschichte und Verwaltung Aegyptens unter Romischer Herrschaft.* Stuttgart, 1915.

Chapters 2 and 3

Albright, W.F., *The Archaeology of Palestine,* London. 1949.

Amélineau, E., *La Géographie de l'Egypte à l'Epoque Copte.* Paris, 1893.

Anon., *The Apocryphal New Testament, being all the Gospels, Epistles and other pieces extant.* London, n.d.

Antoninus Martyr, "Of the Holy Land visited." *PPTS, II.*

Baedeker, Karl, *Egypt and the Sudan.* Leipzig, 1941.

Basset, René, "Le Synaxaire Arabe Jacobite." *Patrologia Orientalis I, III, XI XVI, XVII.*

Bassi, A., *Pellegrinaggio di Terra Sancta.* Turin, 1854.

Brown, R.H., *The Land of Goshen and the Exodus.* London, 1899.

Budge, E.A.W., *The Book of the Bee.* Oxford, 1886.

Budge, E.A.W., *Cook's Handbook for Egypt and The Egyptian Sudan.* London, 1927.

Budge, E.A.W., *The Book of the Saints of the Ethiopian Church.* 4 vols., Cambridge, 1928.

Burchard of Mount Sion, "Description of the Holy Land." *PPTS, XII.*

Burmester, O.H.E. KHS-, *A Guide to the Ancient Coptic Churches of Cairo.* Cairo, 1955.

Butler, A.J., *Babylon of Egypt.* Oxford, 1914.

Evetts, B.T.A., *The Churches and Monasteries of Egypt and some neighbouring countries, attributed to Abu Saleh, the Armenian.* Oxford, 1895.

Felix Fabri, *Fratris Felicis Fabri Evagatorium.* Stuttgart, 1843-1849.

Ghillebert, *Oeuvres de Ghillebert de Lannoy.* Paris, 1878.

Ibn Iyas, *Histoire des Mamlouks Circassiens.* Cairo, 1945.

James, M.R., *The Apocryphal New Testament.* Oxford, 1924.

Jacques de Vitry, "The History of Jerusalem." *PPTS,XI.*

Jullien, Michael, *L'Egypte, Souvenirs Bibliques et Chrétiens.* Lille, 1891.

Keller, W., *The Bible as History.* New York, 1956.

Le Quien, "L'explication de l'homélie de Zacharie, évêque de Saka," *Oriens Christianus, II.*

Ludolph von Suchem, "Description of the Holy Land." *PPTS, XII.*

Maqrizi, *Description Topographique et Historique de l'Egypte.* Paris, 1900.

Marino Sanuto, "Secrets for True Crusaders." *PPTS, XII.*

Meinardus, Otto, *Monks and Monasteries of the Egyptian Deserts.* Cairo, 1960.

Meistermann, B., *Nouveau Guide de Terre Sainte.* Paris, 1907.

Mingana, A., "Vision of Theophilus, or the Book of the Flight of the Holy

Family into Egypt." *Bulletin of the John Rylands Library, Manchester,* 13, 2, (1929), 383-425.

Pascual de Gayangos, *Biblioteca de Autores Espanoles, desde la formacion del lenguaje hasta nuestros dias.* Madrid, 1884. P.145.

Peeters, Paul, *Evangiles Apocryphes.* Paris, 1914.

Quatremére, M., *Mémoires Geographiques et Historiques sur l'Egypte.* Paris, 1811.

Tafur, Pero, *Travels and Adventures.* London, 1926.

Toussoun, O., *La Géographie de l'Egypte à l'Epoque Arabe.* Cairo, 1926.

Walther, Paul, *Fratris Pauli Waltheri Guglingensis Itinerarium in Terram Sanctam et ed Sanctam Catharinam.* Stuttgart, 1892.

In addition to the bibliographical sources mentioned, I wish to express my gratitude to the following priests of the Coptic Orthodox Church who have offered valuable information. Abuna Daudius of the Church of Mari Girgis, Bilbais; Abuna Ishaq Butrus of the Church of Aba-Nub, Samannud; Abuna Yuhanna 'Abd al-Masih of the Church of the Blessed Virgin Mary, Ma'adi; Abuna Ishaq Hanna and Abuna Matta Mikhail of the Church of the Blessed Virgin Mary, Dair al-Ganus; Abuna Hanna Tadrus and Abuna Girgis Yussuf of the Church of Mari Girgis, Ishnin an-Nassarah; Abuna Quzman al-Muharraqi of the Monastery of the Blessed Virgin Mary (Dair al-Muharraq), Kuskam; Abuna Girgis Bistaurus of the Church of St. Sergius, Babylon (Old Cairo); and Abuna Girgis Murqus of the Church of the Blessed Virgin Mary, Musturud.

Produced by the Printshop of the American University in Cairo Press